FLOATING IS EVERYTHING

FLOATING IS EVERYTHING

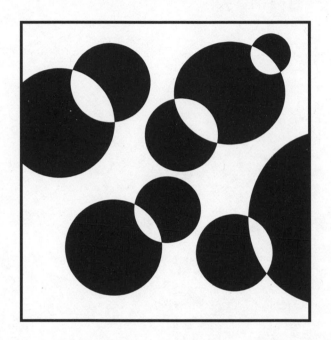

SHERYDA WARRENER

NIGHTWOOD EDITIONS

2015

Nightwood Editions
P.O. Box 1779
Gibsons, BC VON IVO
Canada
www.nightwoodeditions.com

TYPOGRAPHY & DESIGN: Carleton Wilson
COVER IMAGES: Lunar and Planetary Institute

Nightwood Editions acknowledges financial support from the
Government of Canada through the Canada Book Fund and
the Canada Council for the Arts, and from the Province of
British Columbia through the British Columbia Arts Council
and the Book Publisher's Tax Credit.

This book has been produced on 100% post-consumer recycled,
ancient-forest-free paper, processed chlorine-free and printed
with vegetable-based dyes.

Printed and bound in Canada.

CIP data available from Library and Archives Canada.

ISBN 978-0-88971-315-4

for Clyde

Contents

Snare Books Imprint
of
Nightwood Editions
Gibsons, BC V0N 1V0
Canada
www.nightwoodeditions.com

TYPOGRAPHY & DESIGN: Carleton Wilson
COVER: Marijke Friesen and Carleton Wilson

BRITISH COLUMBIA
ARTS COUNCIL

Canada Council   Conseil des Arts
for the Arts   du Canada

Nightwood Editions acknowledges financial support from the
Government of Canada through the Canada Book Fund and
the Canada Council for the Arts, and from the Province of
British Columbia through the British Columbia Arts Council
and the Book Publishing Tax Credit.

This book has been produced on 100% post-consumer recycled
paper, processed chlorine free, and printed with vegetable-based
dyes. Printed and bound in Canada.

CIP data available from Library and Archives Canada.

ISBN 978-0-88971-315-4

A SUDDEN GUST

Elemental

I ace the Myers–Briggs under the high school basement's
lazy fluorescence. Led to a room laddered

with light, the counsellor declares me a knife maker.
Here's the opening I've been waiting for – I climb up

into the bright blueprint of finally knowing.
I'll make tools by hand that last forever: *butcher, table,*

balisong, oyster, palette, modern gravity. I turn
my woodshed into a studio, thread

the sanding machine, envision each piece
passed on as a prized possession for generations. I have it in me

to transform this elemental material, give it purpose, and then
maybe I don't. Do I want this? I'm a Viking.

I take a chunk of obsidian, black guts
of a volcano, forge it into a point

pointing in this direction,
this direction I've been moving all my life.

We Bought a Little City

First, we remove the dreadful yellow awnings from the shop-fronts in the square. Brighten the streetlamps. Play our instruments for the dairy cows crowding the fence. We angle for more daylight, fill out the appropriate paperwork. Get down on hands and knees to clean out the ditches. We eat breaded fish for lunch, drink a cold beer, volunteer to play our part. No one complains of their dreams or dread. A mangy dog comes out of the forest covered in mud and stinking of deep time. Belonging to the old owners, he wants nothing to do with us, knows we'll use him as a bridge: *Look, there he goes with a pheasant in his mouth.* Late October, the windows display ornamental gourds, tidy piles of leaves. Evening in the forest, the eyes and mouths of jack-o'-lanterns spark. A bark, a souvenir. Way off the earth the moon muscles in, entirely invincible.

Dead Air

Baby pulls *Why Are You So Sad?* from the shelf. I tuck it back. Baby pulls it out again, drops it at my feet. I give in, read my favourite poem aloud but leave out the line about horses making love to whales. A wild herd lives on the moon – this impresses him. I shelve the book. He pulls it out, crawls away. I'm the iced grapes brought with the bill, the tetherball's slack rope. Baby eyes the pattern on my coffee cup each time I bring it to my lips. I warn against getting too caught up in it, but what do I know? There's this easygoing part of myself. I'm riding on the back of an old Inuit woman's Ski-Doo. We barrel over snow's erasure until she slows, points to a mound not unlike any other mound. I was expecting a made-up flag or simple notation, a trestle to pass under in fanfare. The too-bright white cascades out in every direction. I bear the silence, dismount, do a little dance while the Ski-Doo idles. Compose life into this moving thing. Not far off, the horses swish and whinny, go about their mutual grooming. Hooves dredge up a dust so particular it suspends in the dead air.

I Am a Winning Personality

"Repetition is not rhyme, missy."
– Elizabeth Bachinsky

I am a winning personality.
My personality is Paleozoic:

sea urchin, horn lantern
with the panes of horn

left out. My personality glows
like a lantern aglow

for the last few million years
or so. My face is alive.

My face is cloudy as a cluster
of cherry blossoms face-down

in a puddle of discarded rain. I pull
up from the dead pile, drenched,

petals intact. At home, a swishy pink
wave from the corner of the room

as the petals dry in the radiator's shunty
updraft. No longer my face,

just a quivering dumb bouquet
with a couple of buds clenched tight

as fists about to fist-bump me. Never
my face in the first place. Everything

will eventually collapse from rain-work
and other festivals of weather unless

I'm there to breathe it in. Herein
lies evidence of my winning personality. I study

the urchin's briny nature for tips
on how to outlast even the chilliest

millennia. *Cold shoulder,*
Baby says, giving me the cold shoulder.

Fortune, Pioneer

So much of measurement
   is the pleasure of going
by feel: eyeball the nail

in the wall and nudge
   the frame left. But
the *Vertical*

Transportation Handbook
   formulates a time x
space tally that leaves our

senses out of it. Dubai,
   Taipei, Shanghai: cities tunnel
upward in the race for

World's Tallest
   until gravity says *No*.
James Fortune, pioneer

consultant, is on the job. Admires
a well-built double decker, the axiom "If
an elevator is in trouble, the safest

place to be is inside
   the elevator." We consider
ourselves lucky

as he weighs car, sheave, shaftway
   with his mind. There's no end
to the vertical possibilities: Transfer

to a second track or
    stop at the seventy-sixth floor for a swim
in the zero-entry pool. Sure,

we'll travel even higher – sky's
    a thing we're sure we'll never
run out of. The arrival prediction

lantern lights up and everyone
    hustles along into the next car, rises
with the temperature. Later

a cab full of passengers falters
    and Fortune finds a way
to ease it back down to Earth.

I wait. Lean
    into window, view, trust
it will hold. Weather

thrashes the glass panels. Fresh
    from the observation deck, here's everything
new for the first time: clouds

doing a bang-up job of instantaneous
    revision, half-moon bay below glittering
like aquamarine rocks stuccoed

onto muslin. What's left
    of invention after this feeling
fails to reinvent itself in time?

Confession

After I tell the one about
the dog and the band saw, everyone's
in the mood to come clean:
K. fed his bulldog acid. M. catapulted
his guinea pig off a queen-size mattress,
breaking its hind legs. "I was only
about eight," S. confesses. "I took
my sister's kitten and wound
it up," (here she uses her hands
like winding a skein of yarn)
"in duct tape. Maybe I thought it would keep
the kitten warm? I was jealous.
Even when I realized what
might happen, I couldn't undo it.
I'd wrapped it over and over
in that mucky grey tape."

I'm sorry I started all this
with a simple punchline.

No matter where you sit at Ryoan-ji,
it's impossible to view the entire
fifteen-rock composition
at once. From the viewing platform
I count and recount the rocks
to be sure. In their groupings
they resemble islands in an ocean,
tiger cubs in the grip
of a mother's teeth, mountain peaks
rising above clouds. What lies
under the faultless white
rake lines? Here's the thing
that's hardest to admit: I'm as cold
as the farthest planet
I've been standing here so long.

Pluto Forever

I

I'm looking at pictures
of Morrissey in a beige
corduroy shirt unbuttoned

to reveal that lithe hairless
chest and think: *Uh oh,*
Nostalgia Land. Who hears

that intro to "How Soon
Is Now?" and doesn't
want to lay down panting

on the carpet? At Kingswood
Amphitheatre, Uncle Paul wore
his homemade *The Smiths*

Are Dead T-shirt and
low-rent Canadian mods
threatened to beat

the shit out of him right
where we sat, summer of '87.
I sang along like I knew

the words: *I am the sun, I am*
the air. Morrissey sent gusts of
wilted gladioli into the front rows, left

the band for a solo career
a year later. Overzealous fans
let *Meat is Murder* spin

into that gravelly, after-album
static. A year later Uncle Paul
flew me to Florida

for my birthday.
Mouse-eared waiters circled
our table holding

sparklers, made me
stand on my chair while
everyone sang.

At the Temple of Doom
we bought a pirate sword
for my brother. Fort Lauderdale

airport security classified
it as a weapon, made us check it
even though there was nothing

else to check.
Uncle Paul was sure it wouldn't make it,
but at carousel D

between a couple of
suitcases, the rubber sword looped
lonely as a whale heart. Remember

when Pluto used to be
a planet? It fails to "clear
the neighborhood"

of its orbit and BLAMMO
we're back to eight. When I
think I might miss

this table, this
view, I may actually
recall only

the little apparatus
I jam under the window
to hold it open.

II

Alouette, the first
Canadian satellite. "Alouette,"
the song Sarah Farrar

and I learned by heart
for grade four French. We
made our own skylark

with removable feathers
and as we sang, *gentille Alouette,*
je te plumerai, we

let the black strips of paper
float to the floor. Who knows why
we call to mind these

moments or how. *Et le
cou (et le cou) et le dos (et le dos)*
lovely little skylark I shall

pluck you.

III

I invite Marco from
next door and Kerri, Luke
and Rob from around

the front to our yard
for my brother's fourth birthday.
Even at ten I have a problem

with occasions going
unnoticed. Mom runs out
for cake, plastic cups,

jugs of Five Alive. I have
everyone sitting on a blanket
waiting when she returns.

There's that look again, but
I don't care. My heart's
chock-full as she walks out

with the cake lit up,
the screen door slamming
behind her.

IV

In Tokyo, I circle
the back streets of Daikanyama
looking for Mama Tarte,

the rambling bakeshop
Yuko used to take me to. Domed
glass case of cakes

we'd stand at a long time
before choosing. I'm forcing
nostalgia onto a plate

of old-fashioned apple pie
but amid the square
concrete blocks of white

the green wooden house
with the glassed-in porch is not
where I knew it to be.

I sit by the Meguro
River and sob fitfully into my No. 1 beer
under a frenzy of petals

like castoff fortunes.
Behind me, two kids out to
make some yen build a Plinko game

out of plywood and nails,
set it up in their garage. Winning
makes me feel even worse.

I give back the prizes
in the end. The river isn't even
really a river, it's more like

an aqueduct, but
the crowds filter in
by the hundreds

with their cameras, zoom in.
Blossoms brief as life. My chest
lifts like a page from

the daily calendar I've forgotten
to rip off. Yuko made me a drawing
of her heart covered

with curly hair
and said, "This is why I live
alone." *Just like*

everybody else does, I think
to myself. Plutino, dwarf
planet 134340,

never mind definitions.
Keep spinning along that restless
path dragging stellar

remnants and other dark
matter into your gravitational
pull. Pluto, I won't

forget you.

A Sudden Gust

After *A Sudden Gust of Wind* (*after Hokusai*) by Jeff Wall

Forget about Hokusai for a minute: in this photograph,
the bend of the tree is a replica of the bend

of the river. A woman loses her headscarf.
A businessman and a farmer crouch into

the wind. Loose-leaf whipped from
a briefcase whirls upward, tangles

with clouds. No sixteenth-century rice field:

this is a cranberry farm outside
Vancouver, actors lurching into the gust.

A digital composite made
of 100 photographs taken over a year. Nothing

can substitute the single brushstroke of
Fuji, so there's no mountain.

Now, lift a corner and let fly

the part of you that can't help
but destroy things. Disrupt

the tableau with a minor catastrophe

and watch the players clutch
at hats, some semblance of

the original: peasants winding through
dry grass, tissues drawn

from a kimono pocket flying skyward.

What did the woman say to the cloud?
You're the doughy centre to this storm.

The grass whispers, *Rice*

is nice rice is nice. Heart and mind
agree on one thing: when seeking a pattern, subvert

the pattern. Ancient Indonesian temple-makers always

turned one stone's marking in the opposite
direction. Nothing's perfect is what

the stars declared, and Borobudur
is circumambulated to this day. This poem

is spliced together from a hundred thoughts, most likely
a modern version of some old idea.

Like the man whose toupée is whipped off, we need to
get over ourselves. Let the wind separate us

from our belongings. Walk empty-minded

into the cranberries and rainwater. Look how
the rectangles of paper become sky! It makes sense now

why the mountain's not there. *Irreplaceable*,
we say to our disoriented selves, this landscape backdrop.

TRACE OBJECT

A Sudden Gust

After A Sudden Gust of Wind (after Hokusai) by Jeff Wall

Forget about Hokusai for a minute: in this photograph,
the bend of the tree is a replica of the bend

of the river. A woman loses her headscarf.
A businessman and a farmer crouch into

the wind. Loose-leaf whipped from
a briefcase whirls upward, tangles

with clouds. No sixteenth-century rice field,

this is a cranberry farm outside
Vancouver, actors leaning into the gust:

a digital composite made
of 100 photographs taken over a year. Nothing

to substitute the single brushstroke of
Fuji, so there's no mountain.

No: lift a corner and let fly

the part of you that can't help
but destroy things. Disrupt

an autumn with a minor catastrophe

Trace Object

"Alles hat ein Ende, nur die wurst hat zwei." *All things come to an end; only the sausage has two.* Her favourite expression. She makes her way around the house with a roll of tape and black marker. The scratch sound as she peels off the roll, a kind of relief. In her cursive my name, my father's name, his brother's name. Turn this or that over, a little death lets out. Birch trees in the front yard smooth, silver-white. Leaves blowing upward reveal their blank undersides.

Sunday brunch table set: runner
with hand-knit edges, plates of fresh
meats, basket of rye, squat tin of
liverwurst turned

onto fine china. *Fleisch salade*,
the good butter. Conversation: will
and testament. Plots

selected. A proper burial. *There go
the Percys,* she interjects, fake
wave out the bay window. *Just
look at him in those shorts.*

She claims when she walks down the stairs her father's cigar smoke hangs there, blue bruised air. Utterly untraceable. Who will inherit the black and white photograph of the ghost that leans against the mirror behind the bar? Alone in the house, I hear my father's guitar up through the vents. What's worse, we haven't lived together for years. And now Baby calling my name through the shower's steam and even he's not here. Who inherits the sound when I'm no longer around?

I take a chance, pretend I'm *off*
to the loo, take the stairs two
at a time. Decisions about
death I want nothing

to do with. On the bureau sits
a porcelain figure, 1920s flapper
in an airy blue dress. I turn

her upside down. A piece
of tape, and written in black,
my name. I settle her back into
her circle of dust.

This porcelain plate's pattern floats up from the plate. Table runner's knit edge uncouples. Intricate lathe scroll work in the shelf he built to hold the Royal Crown Derby paperweights: hedgehog, mountain bluebird. Hand-painted twenty-two-karat gilded geometrics. Who knows what else: band saw, settee, teak ice bucket from behind the bar. An underside to everything. Death staring up blank-faced from a stack of khaki pants.

He'd been giving away
stuff for years from behind
the veneer bar: a hand-carved
horse, leather manicure set

with combed velvet interior,
tools with faux pearl handles.
What did you give her that for?

when she found him out. To make up
for his lack of ceremony, she shoved
her first diamond ring at me, a look
that said, *Don't tell the others.*

Patterns loosen, collapse. Floating gold and black diamonds shimmer unhinged from their place in the world's effortless pattern. Fill in with new. Shortly after he died, she sat on the corner sofa watching *Wheel of Fortune*. Turned toward the nothing that was once her husband and said, *Hello Love.* There's an underside to everything! She's sure he called from his cellphone, and when she slid open the patio door he was there at the corner of the lawn looking back at her. Into his phone he's saying, *I know what you did.* Meaning he watched her get rid of all his shoes and he's not happy about it.

Downstairs they've shifted
to other topics: a new service
road's going in, rain this week, *pass
the trifle. Did you hear?*

*Your cousin's having a lap-band
put in, can't stop himself from eating.
Sad, really. Tuesday, went*

*to have my fortune told,
says he wants to know why
I haven't been wearing the ruby
he gave me!* She makes

a beeline from kitchen
to dining room, talking the whole time.
Tea or coffee? One son says,
Yes. She pours

both into his cup. *Father!*
she says to the empty
chair at the end of the table: *Tell
your son to behave.*

Wind collapses the birch leaves like a magic trick. Clouds clutter up the sky with the ability to shift shape-wise, to be curiously indescribable except to point and say, *A shape in the sky like applause, it floated there.* Absence accumulates. We pretend to no longer notice. Orchid plants flourish like a new language in the bay window, living white and pink petroglyphs.

Reincarnation Study 1982

Of the 122 responses, *trapeze
artist, aardvark, champion logger* and *Teflon coating*

suffer the least lacklustre. Three people claimed
to want to come back as tennis players. A handful

had their assistants type up a note declining
the request: either too overwhelming

a thought, or no one wanted it bad enough. I'm gunning
for permanence. I want to be rigged

taut as a mainsail, blown out with wind. Cut loose
like a satellite into graveyard orbit. Night-blooming

saguaro cactus. Gravity. A corner of the sea
in *Landscape with the Fall*

of Icarus. Let me be kicked
back alive as the red dirt under horse hooves

at Hastings Park. When I start to think
about it hard, sudden circles of death descend

in layers like a Venn diagram. I don't know
what to make of the space where those circles

overlap. Whatever giant paperweight
tamps us down, it isn't sky.

Half-Deflated Heart Balloon

In his dreams

Baby's crying I've taken away

the thing he wants but can't

reach or name A half-deflated heart

floats above the table

Helium performs a final feat

before the whole enterprise depletes For now

it tinges the light red

Baby screams knowing the thing

he wants is hanging

in air like a heart balloon I'll reach out

for the tail-end Baby Just give me

ten more minutes okay? A poem is

a way of dreaming after what

I want and can't have I don't even

know how this thing got here we inherited

this balloon like every wish or hope

that crosses the threshold

like please don't or like please

don't trip on the escalator Baby please

What's wanting without

that dangling thing or the deflated

look of it We can make a game

of grasping as it flies

away Play at the determination

of wanting a thing that's easy

because we're inside with a ceiling

What's hard is the hook of the nearly never

enough And when I hold in my hands

the thing I want belonging now

to me of course I don't

want it any more like this heart balloon

a wounded animal lumbering a half-inch

above the ground I want it out of here

and this Baby I like just fine

but sometimes he could go too or the way I am

with him I don't want to be that thing

he reaches for and can't get at

and this poem too I don't want this

poem I want nothing to do with it

but it belongs to me

Many Tiny Pagoda

In a poem about beauty, a mention
of paper, because isn't paper sad? Origami cranes
slide through water toward us, upright

and industrial, catching mid-
stream on mulch islands only to let go again,
weighed down with nothing

more than a wish that will only last
so long. Just past the bend, a man in white gloves
removes each waterlogged bird out of sight

of its maker. Dusk, we find a spot on the patio
overlooking the river, share a beer under the glow
of many tiny pagoda lanterns

strung above our heads. I resolved not to
place my fortune at the hands of the river, instead
spent the afternoon marvelling at great

wooden structures. Even pagoda five tiers
high, with intricate layers of multiple eaves, will not
topple in an earthquake, remain infinitely

intact. An invisible central pillar allows
for sway, like a willow. This the only safe bet
for hundreds of miles. On site, a custodian

swept gingko leaves from the stone path.
Someone comes now carrying a plate of dumplings,
each dough-edge pinched, fanned by hand.

Paper partitions dividing us
from our neighbors distort nothing. Meticulous
cranes bob along endlessly with an air

of confidence I may never fully possess.
For now, we settle on the pre-verbal sense
the river makes. It tells us all we need to know.

know how this thing got here we inherited

this balloon like every wish or hope

that crossed the threshold

like please don't cry like please

don't trip on the escalator Baby please

What's wanting without

that dangling thing or the deflated

look of it We can make a game

of grasping as it flies

away Play at the determination

of wanting a thing that's easy

because we're made with a ceiling

that's hand is the hook of the nearly never

enough And when I hold in my hands

the thing I want held someone new

to me of course I don't

want it still a sail like this heart balloon

LONG DISTANCE

It's a poem about beauty, a question
of paper because its 'flowers talk.' Origami cranes
slide through water toward an upright

the industrial crushing pad
stamps out lunch islands only to let go again
...

more is the way she touched my hair just
before, he tied his hands, a man in white gloves
caresses each white-handled shirt out of sight

in his makeshift diary we sfteflseytet on the page
overlooking the river channel beauty, under the glow
of many-tier pagoda lanterns

strong in beauty unrivalled, I resolved not to
place my fortune at the hands of the river, instead
spent the afternoon marvelling at great

wooden structures. Even pagoda five tiers
high, with multiple layers of multiple eaves, will not
topple in an earthquake, remain infinitely

intact. An invisible central pillar allows
for sway, like a willow. This the only safe bet
for hundreds of miles. On site, a custodian

Tectonic

In the basement of the National Gallery of Iceland,
sixty-nine black and white photographs, the complete *Untitled
Film Stills*.

I had no idea the prints were so small. Outside, ashfall
from Eyjafjallajökull blows in, bits of pulverized rock and glass

from the recent eruption. Volcano weather and the late-night
light disorient me, even though I've prepared

for both. Of making art, Sherman says, "You start out
your day totally unaware of what's in store." The sky rearranges

my expectations. When the guests complain about delays,
inconvenience,
our host is incredulous: "How can you be so stupid? You're
watching

the way our Earth was formed!" After the exhibit, we climb
the hill overlooking the harbour. False clouds dumb down

the light, our natural instincts. Banks of ash from the east leave
a residue on our clothes, grit in our throats. Tectonic.

Angelique takes a photo of me on a bench holding a beer. At
home, looking
at this picture, I'm surprised by my surprise at how it's turned out.

Ghost Hunters

Tonight, electromagnetic fields
throughout Alcatraz are being measured for paranormal
    activity. To *haunt* is to *trouble, recur,*

lead home. All fun and games until Mom shadows
in to divulge her darkest: my brother's a ghost, trapped between
    worlds. By watching this show she says I'm causing

him pain. I snap the TV off, blank black punctuation.
One of the worst girls in my class said, *Want to know the truth*
    about human compassion? See who

sends a card when someone close to you dies.
When the time came, I kept count. For a while, it was like living in
    one of those CN Tower pens, elevator climbing

when flipped upside-down, quick drop when righted.
Two years later, not much to detect except minor things sadden
    me: a woman on the bus applying lipstick

with a miniature brush; wooden signs hanging
from the branches of fruit trees – *McIntosh 1901; Discovery 1908.*
    How even the smallest mirror adds depth to a room.

His ashes were divided, three urns. We couldn't
decide where to leave him, each of us with our own final scenery
    in mind. Sometimes I hear him

playing his guitar. What I thought would spook
me out I actually like, this deeper kind of listening. Like holding
an ear against someone's jaw while they chew,

revealing another layer, daringly close.

Oh, Yoko

Imagine on repeat on the record player.

Front cover, a polaroid of a man's head inside

a cloud. Back cover, a photograph taken by

a woman whose husband will wrap his body around her body

in the famous picture by Leibovitz circa 1981

wearing a black sweater and jeans while he's naked

just hours before he's shot, and still no one knows

what to think about it. In Tokyo, a red rotary telephone

floats on a plinth in the middle of the exhibit space.

The label on the wall reads, *At any moment, Ms. Ono*

might call. When the phone rings, if the phone rings,

what would her voice sound like? A cloud wrung

inside out, a cloud with her husband's face inside.

Vibrations travelling thousands of miles

through wire, frequencies transmitted without

our knowing, only to arrive. I pull on

a black sweater and jeans in solidarity.

My son, three, wants "Oh Yoko!" again, makes a performance

of singing along. There are things he does

and doesn't understand. His voice lags a little behind,

but in the early morning dark he's got that hopeful

human feeling right.

Dark Matter

At any
one time over
a thousand active
satellites surround
the earth. We rely on
their output, use photos
as screen savers. Apparatus
tightening a noose, or
a tool set in motion
to free us. Here, wisps
of a hurricane
nestle in, bound
for the coast two years
from now. Telescope
data reinvented as advent
calendar. Day twelve:
Asymmetric Spiral Galaxy
with Displaced Core.
Sure, you could say
that's my heart. For relief
we get together, circle
the aboveground
all in the same
direction. One
by one we lift
our feet. No one
asks how far
a current like this
might take us.

Long Distance

"Go on,

wax beautiful

about what makes the world,

glorious bastard years."

– Mark Bibbins

PROLOGUE

On April 12, 1961, Soviet cosmonaut Yuri Gagarin became the first human to travel to space. His orbit around the Earth lasted a total of 108 minutes. He received many honours for his achievement, and attained instant international celebrity.

On March 27, 1968, during a routine training flight, Gagarin's jet crashed, resulting in his death. He was thirty-four years old.

Commander Valeri Polyakov holds the world record for longest single human spaceflight in history, from January 8, 1994, to March 22, 1995, a total of 438 days. Cumulatively, Polyakov spent 678 days in space. He retired in June 1995.

There is no record of the two cosmonauts ever meeting.

I

"How strange and wonderful is life!"
  – Dean Young

Kazakhstan spring-like
despite a fine mantle of snow.
Earth's dimmer switch dismantled.

Smashed light. I disembark
from the shuttle, walk to a lawn chair
at ten paces. This is considered a real feat.

My assistant brings me glasses,
places them on my face even.
I snatch a cigarette straight

from a comrade's hand, demand
a whiskey, neat. Changed in the ordinary
ways: 438 days in space, feet soft

as an infant's. A noiseless
grinding comes to mind, I push it aside.
Base of the radio tower

obscured by fog so the top floats
like a satellite. Cameras flare
behind media lines.

With no one
around to negate the sound,
it sticks around.

II

*"What a strange and magnificent idea glass is –
to be close without being struck..."*
– Tomas Tranströmer, "Icelandic Hurricane"

Accustomed to the *kayutka*
(size of a phone booth, tethered
sleeping bag, fold-out

desk, my own private
porthole) I prefer the cramped space
between radiator and kitchen table,

rely on my place here, a stakeout
over apartment roofs, scaffolding, wires.
Across the way, two men shunt

shoulders of ice and snow
down to the walkway below
with a wallop. My senses

disabled, I tune in
to the dishes drying, suspended
in their rack. Winter stew

like licking a battery. My hollow
shoes in the front hall smuggle
in a darkness. I kick them

out of sight. Eavesdrop on
the furniture: *Ottoman, what do you have
to say for yourself?* Dark by 15:04,

the city's a giant
pinball game, moon a captive
ball in the playfield, and I haven't

a single shot to take. I feel
my internal organs shrinking by 0.0008%,
bone density disintegrating under constant

strike of gravity. Decrease in plasma
volume, calcification of soft tissue,
disruption of taste.

Muscle atrophy. I maintain,
from a professional standpoint, humans
are more than capable of withstanding

unearthly pressures. I'm living
proof. I could have stayed a million
more days and a million more days

were never possible. Even
the sugar bowl here at my elbow
laughs and laughs.

Today is made of a million silver hooks perturbing the sky. Bright imperceptible hooks snag air. Rain multiplies, turns to snow, and the artless algorithm of memory performs its one good trick: boy with a book in his lap, mother and father ghosting the pages, the world outside revealing a stubborn arctic temperament. A man adrift in space. We dropped everything to listen, broadcast alive in every home across the nation: *Everything perfectly working.* Alas, here comes the swift hook of the ongoing present to yank me out of it. A threat hollered across an alleyway, though the name called belongs to someone else. Clouds march on, pulled along by some unearthly force. Yes, the present is inescapable, yet what the mind can bring forward without a second's notice! Moments of my life set off like neon flares. A voice calls me to assist with the upward motion of a zipper, hook-and-eye of a floral dress holding it all together. A day in the park, human pyramid assembling before our eyes, we stop to watch the bare arms and legs of girls clambering up. A feat of the early spring. Crowd gathering at the base. Whatever holds those girls upright before our eyes is an invisible hook of immense proportions. The kind of answer one might rummage for when asking, *Is this all there is?* Yes, and no. Eventually, the pyramid tumbles apart. I half-expected the world to reveal something of itself to me just now but it's only the miniscule hooks of the imagination rearranging air.

III

"Everything that ever happened to me
is just hanging – crushed
and sparkling – in the air,
waiting to happen to you."
– Mary Ruefle, "Saga"

Descendant of 1930s Moscow: decades of endless
streamers embellish Red Square.

Frankfurter a symbol
of abundance. Gorky Street alive
with stalls: live carp,

mirror carp, bream, pike, pink ham, marble bacon,
confectionary pastries, two hundred types
of candies, meats in refrigerated cases.

Bolts of Boston cloth, cheviot, fine
broadcloth. Pavilions, kiosks,
dance floors in the park. A bookstore

on Kirov Street! Heyday of the Moscow Hotel
and now the leather wingbacks are torn, bevelled glass
corroding at the edges. Vodka

mediocre at best. I pay a girl to replace
each drink with an unsullied glass. She's lovely
and discrete. The Old World eclipsed

by the New. Photographs, clippings
of Commander Gagarin charming
as a jackal above the fire.

Too proud to wipe the lipstick stain
of Lollobrigada's kiss from his cheek.
I play along, know I'm next.

Fellow *bogatyrs*, I join you
in your ranks. In our shared space
language, I salute you.

Even the glaciers
nearing their own extinction
wish me well.

IV

"I'm awful at fly-fishing. Terrible.
I just like standing in the river."
    – David Letterman

How dead set
on living I've become.
At the Surrealist exhibit I stumble
upon a mirror maze. A girl of about five
uncouples beside me in a thousand
reflections. "Look," she says. "We're face
to face with all our ancestors!"
And then she's gone.
Magritte's window is a painting
of a painting. From my vantage
point, Earth is nothing like Earth.
I make a move: possibility
or dead end, I'm about to find out.

Today is made of ties, leashes, leads, reins, ropes, fetters, trusses. Tethers of leather, rope, wire, string, nylon, twine, silk. I fasten the refrain of a question to the ongoing present. *Is this all there is?* towed behind a plane on an aerial banner. Routine tactical exercises of an air assault unit, chute strings detangling in unison in mid-air. Uniform at Star City deflates on a shelf, ankle tether disengaged. A bridge, bowstring or cable-stayed, holds. Chain, gold band, cufflink, pewter lapel pin. Escalator's run-on sentence. Clotheslines of listless white sheets. Promotional balloons tied to iron railings. Trains, blood, fucking, on and on. Flag of seaweed jimmied to a stick, jammed into the sandcastle's keep. The moat, the drawbridge. A trapeze floating over the prow of the sailboat – strapped in, I chase my shadow further out to sea. Leashed, an arctic tern bitter with snow-crusted beak hammers this ice-broth for fish. Turns out there were arrows all along: the kick-pleat inverted V of a woman's skirt slightly askew as she walks away; a line of fluorescent triangles delineating the construction of a future I never fully believed would arrive. Thinking this might be an answer to a question, coming up with nothing.

V

Look up. Our lives prototyped
in ancient generations of stars, projected
amidst the cosmic debris

of our own making. Circle,
being circled: that was my life once.
Sixteen sunrises and sunsets a day,

blasts you couldn't draw
a shade to. Off-times, I fiddled
with the ham radio,

certain I heard Gagarin's voice
once or twice. Ever the romantic, all halos
and rainbows, *floating*

is everything. I'm the pragmatic one,
though once when I was working
outside *Mir*, relying on

microgravity and a low-grade harness
to keep me from being sucked out into stratosphere,
I turned my headlamp off, stuck an arm out

into total darkness and (I'll admit
it now) there's no way to describe how
suddenly that arm vanishes. At home,

arias echo inside the light well.
I continue to make whole parts
of myself disappear.

Pull a lever and my legs float up.

VI

"I've been feeling kind of temporary."
– Willy Loman, *Death of a Salesman*

Each time I leave my home
someone stops me on the street,
waits for my expression

to flip like a Tarot card
in their favour. I could differentiate layers
of landscape, it was possible even

to determine the direction
of the motion of the sea. Rivers fan out
darkly from cities, straggler stars

rejuvenate by adopting fresh matter
from companion stars. Stacks of galaxies
tens of thousands of light years away,

irregular moon, dark hinging
on dark and yes, I wished for my name
to be spelled out in the Marquis

on Broadway: *Polyakov, Columbus
of Space!* Flash mob signalling me home
with nine million lighters aglow,

fireworks over the Cosmodrome.
Don't despair. My Earth Sadness Ratings
are on par with where they fell before.

I check the boxes beside
balanced, distracted, bored,
and *happy* – this is my job.

VII

"Look more closely from farther away."
– Tsuruhiko Kiuchi, astronomer

Road to Star City
mistaken for logger's track,
farm route. A universe

incongruent with a boyhood
universe, astronomy guide open and me,
giddy as a dashboard ornament,

looking through the collapsible
clouded eye of my telescope,
taking notes and comparing

to those I find in a magazine
for amateurs: Long Eye, Little One,
Psychedelic Zebra.

April 12, 1961, is a pinhole
our whole nation slid through
like a sliver into sky.

108 minutes a crystalline
loop. Everyone dropped everything
to listen. Landing blown

off course, Gagarin parachutes
the seven remaining kilometres, lands
on the bank of the Volga.

That same day, Kennedy
throws a hard fastball across
the plate to commence

the 1961 Major League Season
but there was no going back.
The water within the wave

is not the wave itself
and will be left behind.

VIII

"I want the whole world to be new!"
– James Tate

I circle the window
or the window frames me in its frame.
No future or past, I'm capable

of stopping time just
by setting down my tumbler
on its leather coaster.

Invisible flight path
above the adjacent roofline. Blue tracks
in snow, passers-by and the girl

at Texas Burger Co. unstacks
chairs as she does every afternoon at this time.
Fallen into a pattern

as familiar as wallpaper, I'm still
there as she restacks at the end of her shift.
At 02:00, glass shatters

around a man smashing
his body back through a hole
he's made in the bar window,

bottles tucked under his arms
like newly acquired wings. I watch
as a new pane is delivered

and installed by noon the next day.

Today is made of holding patterns. Discernable flight path above the apartment across the way, ducks stuck in wallpaper angling for a way out, parquet, armchair plaid. Clouds defeating the laws of gravity by floating unpredictably on, casting anvil-shaped shadows. Stereogram of rain: I adjust my eyes and out jumps a shark! Geraniums recur in window boxes, half-hearted red arguments against the grey. The shark refuses call-back; I train my eyes elsewhere. Traffic, advertisements, domestic debris. Walking through the streets, I beg the world to redeem itself like a coupon with no foreseen expiration. Pop music from a loudspeaker assures me with its refrain. At the café, I wonder at the miniature elevator delivering coffee to the tenants above, a performance piece I call *Rising Up Against All Odds*. Just when I think I've understood something about the world, the elevator descends, shudders open and it's empty. Add this hearty dose of disappointment to the party, the party favour, the striped dome of the umbrella stabbed into a maraschino cherry. Elaborate structure of pastel macarons. Shoe pattern, pattern-maker, a cheeseburger in the hands of a teenager. Back at the window, stars outnumber streetlights and there's a reassurance to that fact. City's fibre optics on a timed loop. Black asterisk on the page its own smashed galaxy, cold as a diamond cut from a planet made entirely of diamond. No surprise when that jaunty refrain forces its way back.

IX

I filled the brief, made tidy
this human experiment. Aced
the exams. Now, Gagarin

and I make a dark
pair. I have nowhere
I would rather be

than here. Never made aware
of something so clear, I let go.
When I dream, the air

is smooth as the lining of a fox fur coat.
I'm at the market, vendors calling out,
"Hello Gorgeous!" holding up bags

of the thing I want and they're full.

X

*"Each thing has acquired a new shadow behind the usual shadow
and you hear it trailing along even in total darkness."*
– Tomas Tranströmer

Farthest object ever
observed: a quasar ten billion
light years away,

brighter than one hundred
normal galaxies. Close up:
marble sill, lop-

sided jade, crumbs.
Apartment building
windows. Sloped

roof, snow. Drain
pipe's reverse crown
of ice. Antennae,

satellite dish, piping,
metal box. Cloud scaffolding,
sky scaffolding, pure sky.

Old stove's pilot light
ticks at my back. Opera
ghosts in from behind

the fridge. My neighbour
singing or a recording, I miss
it when it's not there.

Petit Pichet

At La Closerie des Lilas we sit
    at the mirror where Jean-Paul and Simone

once lingered across from their reflections
    drinking until one or the other

would lean over and say, "Let's go upstairs."
    Man Ray winks out at us. They're all ghosts now –

names tamped into brass plates – but the red and blue boats
    at Jardin de Luxembourg are real.

The children pushing the boats around
    the fountain with wooden poles are alive.

The Euros that pay for our olives are real.
    Ghosts walk in and out; no bother. I don't

want to talk about death. At Musée d'Orsay,
    Olympia, black ribbon tied at her throat, isn't

bathing or dreaming or dressing. She's here,
    orders a drink, a castoff

slipper under her stool, orchid
    in her hair.

*

At Centre Pompidou, Sophie Calle's photographs
    of a New York phone booth are alive. She's painted

the booth green, stencilled the word ENJOY
    up one side, decorated with a bouquet

of flowers, a few trashy novels.
    From her lawn chair outside the booth, she gives away

sandwiches, packs of cigarettes. On the placard,
    her findings: *125 smiles given for 72 received... 1 shared burst*

of laughter. I walk away from the installation with the intention
    of improving my life. As if no one's steering, drift

like a sailboat through the St. Martin canal locks.
    The man with the mustache who flirts with us

while loading chickens onto the spit
    of his sidewalk rotisserie is alive.

*

Neon lilacs glow above the patio. Sun silvers the green
    bridge. Later, we'll watch

homecomers exit the Patisserie biting down hard
    on the crusty tips of baguettes. Later, a waitress

will bring us a giant glass bowl of pudding and we'll use the spoon
    she provides to help ourselves. For now, mid-afternoon,

over a shared plate of olives, our clouded *pastis*, a *petit pichet*
    of ice water to dilute the drinks, we act as alive

as ever. Our reflections in the mirror remain
    intact. From the bar, Olympia stares us down.

*

It's your idea to purchase the pack from the machine
    on the wall, replace one of the cigarettes

with a rolled note for the bartender, thanking him
    for recommending *Le Fraicheur*, for the reminder

to add the ice water a little at a time, for excusing
    our French, for inviting the ghosts in the mirror

to watch us try at this life, really try.

Letter to Mel from East Van

Just got back
from LA, rented a bungalow in Mar Vista
with a cast iron door frame that seconds as a breezeway
when you unlatch the glass –

We'd be splayed out on the lawn
drinking after a long day of driving, circling, getting lost,
    winding up back where we started
when a grapefruit would drop

    like a sun
out of the sun-dusky air
all hollow pith and yellow peel.

File this under LA sounds,
along with the rustle of palm husks struck
by cars like roadkill, the voice

of the guy on the boardwalk in full uniform,
sign at his feet that reads *Free Hugs,* claiming

"People'll spend $1.50 on a coffee at Starbucks over a chance
to hug a former soldier. That's true." So far, no takers.

    We get out of Venice Beach fast –

past the mint-green façades of abandoned
    beach resorts, retro signage for *Continental Terrace* or
    Bob's BIG BOY *Original Double Deck Hamburger.*

Faux-adobe homes stucco the arid hills.
I can't seem to shake the fact that a young Didion
is staring out from any number of ocean-front
    patios with that unequivocal glare through dark glasses.

No surprise she's here. A drought, nothing left
    in the San Bernardino groundwater basin,
and she's ordering mussels for 12 or 25,
sipping cocktails at the appropriate hour knowing
everyone, everyone's thirsty.

South to San Onofre, or north to Malibu,
        squadrons of brown pelicans glide above the surf
in V-formation, unremarkable to locals. Persistent
    as Morse code, they punctuate air.

The surfers make it look easy. Nothing's easy. *The point*

is not to quit. So says this poet
I'm reading, likened to ace flyer Florence Leontine Lowe.
I like to think I'm a Pancho Barnes type too –

even in death she was out for a joyride, ashes
    dumped from an aircraft above the HAPPY BOTTOMS
FLYING CLUB only to catch on a crosswind and sweep

    back up into the Cessna. Turns out
I have a fear of heights that left me stranded

on the high dive New Year's Day,
a panic I didn't know I had whipping in just clear
of the handrails. It took everything

in me to skulk back down the ladder
to the hot tub ramp.

Your own refusal to fly comes to mind.

    In LA it's legal for motorbikes to split
lanes, creep up in between cars and fly off
once the light's gone green. Those guys just scream
    Make it count, don't they?

Dad, I'm gonna go –

    My plastic Happy Cat
waves metronomic from the shelf,
storing up whatever good
fortune floats in the air.

The future. At night, a ticking
I didn't hear before. I dislocate
the tiny golden arm
so I can rest.

Pools in Florida

After *Ginger Shore, Causeway Inn, Tampa, Florida, November 17, 1977*
by Stephen Shore

Never mind that it's November and there's a woman to her waist in it. We can't see the woman's face or maybe it's a girl. Her aquamarine suit ties at the shoulders. Miniature wet bows. The frame of the photograph makes a triangle of ledge and railing. She's looking past the sun chairs reclining toward the natural bay. The pool water is cheerful, no one's arguing against that. The auburn of the girl's hair and skin makes for great proximity effect. Does she feel lonely? Dusty rose of the bay in the distance, bright sunburst pattern on the surface of the pool. Yes, she's longing to be elsewhere. Just past the sun deck there's something invisible worth having.

Letter to Mel from East Van

    Just got back
from LA. rented a bungalow in Mar Vista
with a cast iron door frame that seconds as a breezeway
when you unlatch the glass—

We'd be splayed out on the lawn,
drinking after a long day of driving, circling, getting lost,
    winding up back where we started
when a grapefruit would drop

    like a note
out of the sun-dusky air
all hollow pith and yellow peel

rate this under ... sounds,
along with the rustle of palm husks struck
by cars like roadkill, the voice

of the guy on the boardwalk in full uniform,
... a his ... that reads: *Free Hugs*, claiming

People'll spend $5 on a cup of coffee at Starbucks over a chance
to hug a former soldier. That's true. So far, no takers.

    We got out of Venice Beachfast

... let the mint green facades of abandoned
    ... resorts ... settings for *Courtenay/Terrace* or
    the ... *Spiritual Republic Daily Hangover*

Notes on the Poems

This collection quotes Commander Yuri Gagarin's translated transmission from space, from the documentary *First Orbit* by Christopher Riley.

ELEMENTAL is for Cedar Bowers, with thanks for the real-life anecdote that inspired the poem.

DEAD AIR cites the title of the selected poems of David W. McFadden.

FORTUNE, PIONEER was inspired by the article "Up and Then Down" by Nick Paumgarten in the April 21, 2008, issue of the *The New Yorker*.

PLUTO FOREVER is for Lindsay Cuff.

TRACE OBJECT is for my grandmother.

REINCARNATION STUDY 1982 shares its title with an art publication cataloguing the responses to the survey question, *If reincarnation were available to you, in what form would you like to return?*

MANY TINY PAGODA takes its title from a line of a poem by Matthew Zapruder.

TECTONIC cites an interview with Cindy Sherman from the *Journal of Contemporary Art*.

OH, YOKO cites an exhibition of Yoko Ono's work in Tokyo, Japan circa 2003.

Long Distance draws from the following articles and books:

Binns, Christopher A.P. "The Changing Face of Power: Revolution and Accommodation in the Development of the Soviet Ceremonial System: Part I." *Man*, New Series, 14:4. (1979): 585–606.

Brovkin, Vladimir. *Russia after Lenin: Politics, Culture and Society, 1921–1929*. New York, NY: Routledge: 1998.

Fitzpatrick, Sheila. *Everyday Stalinism: Ordinary Life in Extraordinary Times: Soviet Russia in the 1930s*. New York, NY: Oxford University Press: 1999.

Petit Pichet is for Heather Jessup. A reference is made to an installation by Sophie Calle, which is an excerpt from *The Gotham Handbook* and is a direct response to a set of instructions posed by novelist Paul Auster, including the question, *Can one ever have a truly authentic experience?*

Letter to Mel from East Van is for my dad, and is written after the poem "Letter to Denny from Brooklyn" by Amanda Smeltz.

Acknowledgements

Grateful acknowledgement is made to the editors of the journals and anthologies in which the following poems first appeared:

The Believer: "A Sudden Gust"
EVENT: "Tectonic"
Hazlitt: "I Am a Winning Personality,"
The Impressment Gang: "Elemental," "Dead Air,"
    "Pools in Florida,"
Lemon Hound: "We Bought a Little City,"
PRISM International: "Reincarnation Study 1982"
PRISM International: "Pluto Forever," also selected for
    Best Canadian Poetry in English 2013
Riddle Fence: "Dark Matter," "Fortune, Pioneer,"
    "Ghost Hunters"

I am grateful to the Canada Council for the Arts for providing funding, and the Baltic Centre for Writers and Translators for offering space. Both were critical to the writing of this book.

Thank you to Silas White for seeing the potential, Carleton Wilson for the design, and the rest of the lovely team at Nightwood.

To my exceptional family and friends, you are in every poem.

Thanks to Liz Bachinsky, who read early drafts of the manuscript and said things like, *This is not a long poem. I'll show you a long poem!* Her tough talk motivated me to take the work light years beyond where it started.

I am indebted to Raoul Fernandes and Laura Matwichuk for their care and generosity as readers of later drafts.

Clyde, may you always be curious, ferociously so.

And to Chris: clear eyes, full hearts, can't lose.